Nature and Human Inventions

Written by Brylee Gibson

CONTENTS

Nature and Human Inventions 2

How Animals and Humans Use Grip 4

How Animals and Humans Keep Safe 8

How Animals and Humans Move Fast 12

How Animals and Humans Find Food 14

Index 17

T0360105

Nature and Human Inventions

Animals have special body parts that help them. They can use their body parts to grip and keep safe. They can use their body parts to move fast through water and find food. Sometimes people need help to do these things, too. So they make inventions that work like animal body parts.

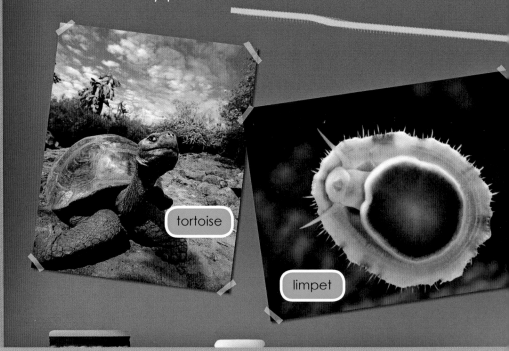

tortoise

limpet

macaw

armadillo

All these animals have special body parts.

squid

How Animals and Humans Use Grip

A limpet is a shellfish that lives on rocks. It holds on to slippery rocks with a suction foot. The limpet won't get washed away by big waves because of its foot.

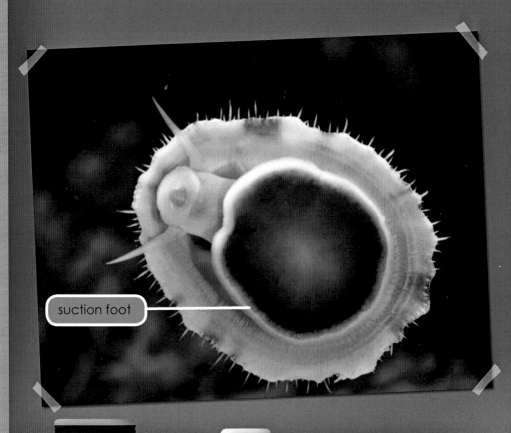

suction foot

This man is climbing a building using suction cups.

A suction cup works just like the limpet's foot. People use suction cups to help put glass windows into buildings. Suction cups can be so strong, people can use them to climb up the sides of buildings!

A cheetah can run very fast when it is chasing its prey. It has long, sharp claws on its feet that stick out all the time. The claws help the cheetah grip dry ground. The cheetah would not be able to run so fast without its claws.

A cheetah can run as fast as 100 km per hour.

long, sharp claws

People who run on tracks can have spikes on their shoes. The spikes are like a cheetah's claws. They grip the track and help the runner go faster.

gripping spikes

How Animals and Humans Keep Safe

Some animals have thick shells to protect them from their enemies. A tortoise has a thick, hard shell on its back. The tortoise can't run fast from its enemies, but it can pull its head and legs into its shell.

The shell helps keep the tortoise safe.

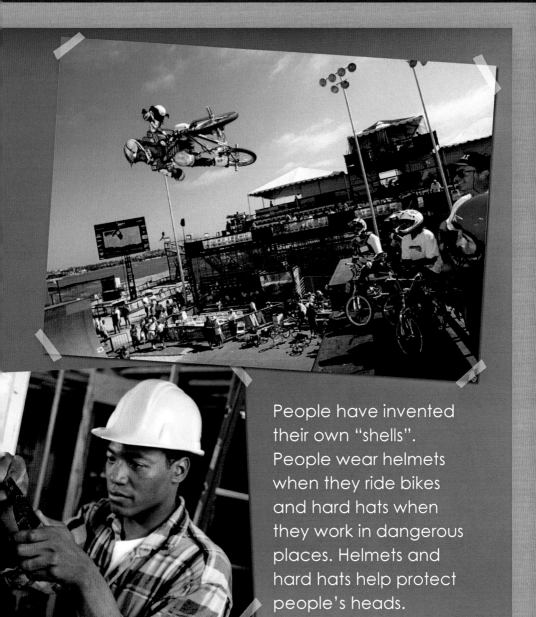

People have invented their own "shells". People wear helmets when they ride bikes and hard hats when they work in dangerous places. Helmets and hard hats help protect people's heads.

Some animals have bony plates to protect them. An armadillo is covered with bony plates. The hard bone plates help keep the armadillo safe from its enemies. The plates overlap, so the armadillo can still move easily. It can roll up into a ball when it is attacked. Its head and legs will be safe.

bony plates that overlap

steel plates that overlap

Knights of long ago had armour like an armadillo. The armour was made of plates of steel that overlapped. The armour was very heavy. But, because it overlapped, the knight was able to bend his arms and legs.

How Animals and Humans Move Fast

Octopuses and squids use water to move fast. They suck water into their bodies. Then they use their strong muscles to squirt it out again. When they want to change direction, they squirt the water a different way. Squids and octopuses can move fast when they are escaping from danger.

An octopus can move as fast as 32 km per hour.

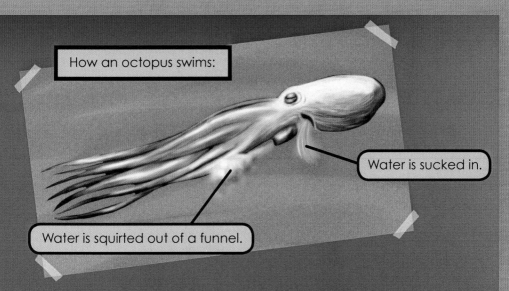

How an octopus swims:

Water is sucked in.

Water is squirted out of a funnel.

A jet boat has an engine that helps it move like octopuses and squids. The engine sucks water in at one end and pushes it out with force at the other end. This helps the jet boat move very fast through the water.

How Animals and Humans Find Food

Some animals use their beaks and jaws to help them get food. This bird uses its strong beak and jaw to crush a nutshell and get the nut out.

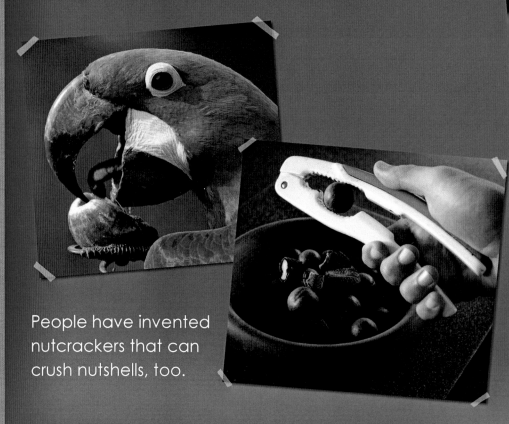

People have invented nutcrackers that can crush nutshells, too.

Young dragonflies like to eat small fish. They have two sharp hooks on their bottom lip. They use these hooks to catch food. When a young dragonfly sees a fish, it flicks out its bottom lip and grips the fish between the two hooks.

People use hooks to catch fish, too. When they are fishing, they flick a fishing line through the water. The hook at the end of the line catches the fish.

There are many other ways that nature and human inventions are alike.

A dandelion seed is like a parachute.

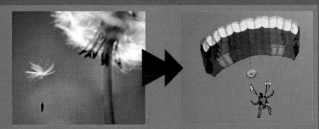

A rattlesnake's rattle is like an alarm. It keeps other animals and people away.

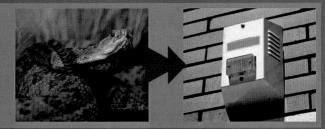

Some whales have rows of thin plates in their mouths that work like a sieve.

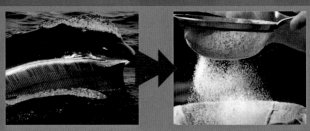

This bird's beak can cut things like scissors.

Index

finding food

    animals 14, 15

    people....................................14, 15

gripping

    animals 4, 6

    people...5, 7

keeping safe

    animals 8, 10

    people.......................................9, 11

moving fast

    animals 12

    people...13

Explanations

Nature and Human Inventions is an Explanation.

An explanation explains how or why things happen.

An explanation has a topic:

Nature and Human Inventions

An explanation has headings:

How Animals and Humans Use Grip

How Animals and Humans Keep Safe

How Animals and Humans Move Fast

How Animals and Humans Find Food

Some information is put under headings.

How Animals and
Humans Use Grip

A limpet holds on to
slippery rocks with a
suction foot.

People use suction
cups to help put glass
windows into buildings.

Information can be shown in other ways.
This explanation has . . .

Labels

Photographs

Captions

Comparison Chart

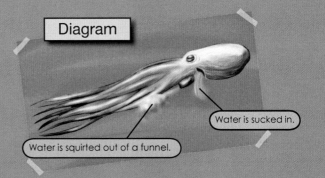

Diagram

Water is sucked in.

Water is squirted out of a funnel.

Guide Notes

Title: **Nature and Human Inventions**
Stage: Fluency

Text Form: Informational Explanation
Approach: Guided Reading
Processes: Thinking Critically, Exploring Language, Processing Information
Written and Visual Focus: Illustrative Diagram, Labels, Captions, Contents Page, Index, Comparison Chart

THINKING CRITICALLY
(sample questions)

Before Reading – Establishing Prior Knowledge
- What do you know about the similarities between animal body parts and human inventions?

Visualising the Text Content
- What might you expect to see in this book?
- What form of writing do you think will be used by the author?

Look at the contents page and index. Encourage the students to think about the information and make predictions about the text content.

After Reading – Interpreting the Text
- Why do you think a person would climb up the side of a building?
- Why do you think a cheetah's claws stay out all the time?
- What are some similarities and differences between a tortoise's shell and a safety helmet?
- Why do you think knights of long ago wore heavy armour?
- Look at the diagram on page 13. How do you think the octopus sucks in the water?
- What things in the book helped you understand the information?
- What questions do you have after reading the text?

EXPLORING LANGUAGE

Terminology
Photograph credits, index, contents page, imprint information, ISBN number

Vocabulary
Clarify: inventions, suction, prey, spikes, overlap, knights, engine, nutcrackers
Nouns: animals, people, cheetah, armadillo, knights
Verbs: climb, run, grip, roll, bend
Singular/plural: person/people, enemy/enemies, body/bodies, dragonfly/dragonflies
Focus the students' attention on **adjectives, homonyms, antonyms** and **synonyms** if appropriate.